amuk

amuk
Khairani Barokka

Nine Arches Press

amuk
Khairani Barokka

ISBN: 978-1-913437-88-6
eISBN: 978-1-913437-89-3

Copyright © Khairani Barokka, 2024.

Cover artwork: © Khairani Barokka, 2024.

All rights reserved. No part of this work may be reproduced, stored or transmitted in any form or by any means, graphic, electronic, recorded or mechanical, without the prior written permission of the publisher.

Khairani Barokka has asserted her right under Section 77 of the Copyright, Designs and Patents Act 1988 to be identified as the author of this work.

First published March 2024 by:

Nine Arches Press
Unit 14, Sir Frank Whittle Business Centre,
Great Central Way, Rugby.
CV21 3XH
United Kingdom

www.ninearchespress.com

Nine Arches Press is supported using public funding by Arts Council England.

for Mitra

Contents

amuk

14

doa

prayer directed at x	70
prayer against the hunt	71
to cleanse in reeds	72
prayer for cave with rectangular light	73
tub	74
(before firewood prays, she hears)	75
lex talionis	76
peace, with c-ptsd	77
prayer doa in which di mano: english inggris, baso minang and dan bahasa indonesia fight berseteru	78
prayer encased in my father's vision of a journey to the afterlife	80
for a jakarta microbiome	81
tsunami warning, facing shore	82
prayer for man in accident, elephant and castle	83
prayer as fistful of praise	84
preceding a prayer for the dead asian men who inspired *a nightmare on elm street*	86
a cartographic hunger	88
prayer for dzikir as mnemonic device	91
matrihaemoglobin	92
prayer for baby breath	94
doa angin / wind prayer:	
1.	96
i trip into gust of sour lung	97
shape of an entreaty	98
theories for sky	99
dust ablution	100
doa tanah / dirt prayer	101
Notes	103
Acknowledgements	104
Cover Description	107

Sometimes all I have
are words and to write them means
they are no longer
prayers but are now animals.
Other people can hunt them.

– *Victoria Chang*

The double vision required to recognize the soul in a badly translated word evinces another way of being in and understanding the world. This dual communication hinges on attunement, which I understand as speaking in order to listen to others, rather than eloquence, listening to yourself.

– *Elisa Taber*

[bahasaku

bahasaku

bahasaku

bahasaku]

my language

my language

my language

my language

in praise of

[   ]

  [   ]

               [   ]

       [**]**

   [   ]

                   [   ]

         [   ]

         [   ]

               [   ]

                         [   ]

i. amuk | اموق

or, what must be felt

or

text from a performance lecture to commemorate the official universe-wide recognition of amuk, amok, and amuck as separate voices in a past-present-future

or

the tail end of a five-hundred-year-old scream, in not-one temporal tense

bok, mungkin perlu kita jelasin dulu ya.

to enter the indonesian language is a science fictional enterprise.

it is a universe of speculative words, gestures, perception.

this work is a move to remind ourselves of this, of these chronotypes.

*

indonesian (not 'bahasa', which simply means 'language', but **bahasa indonesia) has no tenses.**   thus

all translations into english, where past or present or future must be pinned down, as definite, are both potentially right and always wrong.   a reductive *tense* cannot encapsulate the speculative nature of our language. the science fictional possibilities, destabilisations.

and this is, of course, not to mention the other different linguistic cosmologies in the archipelago, over 700 other languages and ways in which neurons enhance possibilities beyond modernity's fixity, persnickity predilection for pinning

                                                     down.

*

linguistic cosmology—
       how stars move and imprint upon the body

translations from bahasa indonesia as illustration (reminder):

kami makan [we eat
              we ate

                        we will eat]

kami kelaparan
                [we starve
              we starved

                        we will starve]

kami mati [we die
            we died

                        we will die]

                      *

the refusal of indonesian
and various indigenous languages
to conform [to have conformed]
              to temporal orthodoxy

is-was-willbe the greatest of wisdoms
on the tips of our tongues and limbs
kept-keeping-will keep self-protecting
                        in the leaves

the following is the story of how continually ruling factions interact with worlds in which they are [certainly were, most likely will not be] not fully aware of how time passes-passed-willpass, in what contexts.

unaware of, or resistant to truths regarding, what they have contributed-contribute-areheadlongtowards futurecontributing to these timeframes. centuries that impact bodyminds—**human, animal, otherwise**—through mitochondrial recall, and retention of affects ancestral that have been-are-willbe brought to bear.

*

ancestrally, we think (thought) of time within different geometries.

a non-linearity. cycles, continuance.

motion passing-passed-willpass steadily past gregorian decades, through indigenous calendars.

this is and was-willbe the story of one such emotion: **amuk**.

and the ways it has been framed, claimed by twisted offspring of variant malevolences.

learning the word as a child—
sense perception:

when a baby **mengamuk**

their fists flail   in hot air
spittle shot through   high decibels
their feet kick the toy truck   violently
away

their fat belly moves   side to side
the giant of their land

*

perhaps another example
from a mind with this word inside it
for decades (centuries, and beyond):

when an adult is led to **mengamuk**
their keyboard is thrown on the desk
in their home where bigboss can't see
that bloodshot eyes and carpal tunnel
have led them to primal scream

rage-raged-willrage, doing, verb

amuk is a clean emotion
an anger so pure it purifies air—
to mengamuk is that rage-release
is that rage-redux in infinite ways

when fingers bring the pixels, in later adulthood, when i search
for what the worlds of english deem is **amuk's** meaning—it
becomes a foreign word to me

with much different stories for this word than i have known,
absorbed from childhood (an infancy filled with tantrums—'dia
mengamuk'—in which i **mengamuk**)

*

thumbswept dictionaries and thesauri
empir(e-)ical

claim different meanings for amuk than i knew before the
stubborn carapace of adulthood had even crept in:

pathologies
murder

but we will come to that.

first, we will let the word speak for itself.

voice-voices (for the singular word form in malay/indonesian can also potentially be plural) of amuk:

in a past-present-future,
there are very many more instances of what definitions of **amuk**
are used for, outside of violence

'eh, tiba-tiba dia ngamuk...'
'ngamuk gimana?'
'gitu lho, teriak-teriak gitu.'

rage plus the thud suddenness: shouting, screaming, flailing.

'sudden', however, may imply that before, there was **nothing** below the surface that brimmed

                     and boiled to
                                       tip
                                                          over.

*

we are kettle-steam screaming

and you, **amok**, are a diagnosis so banal it could only be evil

and you, **amuck**, are a digression of self-certain phrenology and the two of you have been witness to the framing of our non-human relatives as 'nature' by colonial batons and to the maladies peoples have been forced to bear for five hundred years

being heard at the very tail-end of that scream and drowned (a very appropriate word) out.

*

we, the voices of **amuk**, recall the following quote, from yoruba philosopher bayo akomolafe:

> *'what we rudely call 'nature' today does not even have a name in Yoruba culture because there was no distinction between us and the goings-on around us. [...] mountains could be consulted, trees could have privileges...*

this is how babies in now-malaysia and the now-indonesian archipelago were taught, across hundreds upon hundreds of languages. language cosmologies that were all forcibly hunted

hunted at the throat

some to extinction, for all this genius to cower under false mirrors' voices on the brow of a ship.

some hunted people hunt people. the hope of an indonesian government has turned colonial in itself, under the weight of the west's arms and demands post-1965 genocide, itself continues to hunt papua at the throat.

[human voice-voices resume-resumes, in place of amuk's]

amuk i. waters

we [saw
  see
  will see]
           something
                horizon-adjacent:
            the ships

we [smell
  will smell
    smelled]
           the brine

with the waters [came
        come
        will come]
                            newcomers

*

and our language evolved-evolve-evolves
with the passing [ghostly: passed, will pass] of goods through arab
                    chinese
                        gujarati hands

our animist faiths submerge[-d, will submerge] in ganges and in zamzam
water, in yangtze river

our bloodlines crisscross in natal helixes
our stars commingle
materials of the universe create[d, will create] bone and breath
from our wombs
with the inborn memory, submerg-ing(-ed, will be submerged),
of such a span of earthly places

the many kingdoms and many wars in our archipelago
centuries of feet on backs
and the weaving of peoples with place, in opposition

at some point met, meet, will meet, the barrel of shackles brought
by ships

*

the ships say our very flesh is here for profit
—and there is such a thing as 'nature'
and it is not human—
instead of our interweaving lives with all that lives
they introduce us to the cloud of profit
and say that this apparition is what nature is for

and by the way, we are not supposed to be human
                                             either

you want to talk corporate history
look to the world's first proto-megacorp
the dutch east indies company

nearly two million of our bone-and-breath
enslaved by the dutch
over two hundred years
—if not 'merely' indentured labour—

*

adults and children, bought, sold
over two hundred years
require a holding of the breath, in respect
in horror-bright burst of prayer

[   ]

your beloved walks into a black hole
unable to move their limbs
and you hear a splash

*

our bone-and-breath that survive
are in suriname's javanese
in south africa's cape malays
and marked as 'developing world' at home

because the web of fiction
known as capital persists,
our bone-and-breath is-was-willbe in migrant workers
who seldom-never see home waters

accumulation of the fictitious web
—the natural reason for such sanctities as family
to endure these many breaks

our swamps a melee
of molecules thrown into disarray

*

these waters, we are told, are no longer ours [were no longer
ours, are no longer…]

if we fish, we fish for their far-off queens,
and mangroves are not living kin
they are 'natural resources'
to be shipped off

or made into meneer's fortresses
and gallows

on the ocean, our waters are carted to other waters

if you **mengamuk** against empire
if you grasp fully the breath between

[   ]

you and your family
will be shipped away
from the only waters you know
to eat exile
for as long as the sun will taste your skins

on the ship, for them, the waters are [were, will be] calm
for your family, the waters are [will be, were] rageful

                                              brimming

                                                          waiting for release

*

burnt farms throw ash into paddy field water
burnt trees to smoke us out of our forests
fall into rivers and fire meets silt
where sungai meets laut

our animals hunted (will hunt, they hunt them) to burning
for furs and gilded stakes
mounted taxidermy (mounts, it will mount)
      [can they only see themselves reflected
      in the dead-eyed]

and freshwater sheds its skin
as it sees saltwater filled with bodies
and saltwater mirrors springwater
and both amass the spoils of destruction

both haze and iron,
a cloud tells us 'i say when'
'i tell you when you are'

'i say these swamps
are backwaters
and not the fulcrum of your lives

your sciences are not centuries-old
but lint in our peaked hats

this place is nothing but amenities
for our cheery vortex'

*

'you and your many generations
of children will grow
to throw fists and knives for your waters
to be left to their stewards
as we say
these wood supplies are not for stewarding—
at least until the twentieth century

when we say the stewards
are those we must first teach'

both haze and iron,

it is forced down our ears:

'we do not care for the names
of water gods
or indigenous irrigation technologies

wait until your great-grandchildren
get masters in natural resource management
when we can tell you
that we are "developed"
and you can feel for yourself
where that leaves you'

*

'we omit the ladder we place-placed-will place on necks
with a scarf-bundle of debt
gnawing-gnaw-willgnaw at sciatica
and at rivers you used for all your needs,
now filled-fill-willfill with plastic waste
we export-exported-willexport to your country from ours

chemical iron, chemical haze
longstanding, disabling phase
and official phraseology'

'when we wring-willwring our fingers
about the environment, suddenly trendy,
we omit-willomit bulldozers
lolling their maws at the grasshoppers
and dozers' gunpowder antecedents
and written rules of law
that place your fishing boats shrivelled
your oceans soon warmed
and we will claim your ignorance
of any way to ever stop tides of heat'

*

'we will corporate-social-responsibility
your revolutionary indigeneities
and oil slick our way through
the feel-good advertisement landscape'

[iron and haze
care not for how all waterways breathe
with human blood as their inverse
and keeper]

'we omit-haveomitted-willomit marketing you as "paradise"
to hide mass graves
and buying-havingbought-willcontinuetobuy
your paddy fields
against half-millennia of farmer resistance
and fealty to sacred waterways
mowed down for influencer wedding venues
and for your aunts and mothers and daughters
to docilely massage the ankles
of ours
by waters we retain for their sound effects
as heard somewhat faintly
from the spa

we cage your so-called stewardship
of waters'

*

—*iron and haze*—

blood is borne on the sea
an oil rig
births an unending rage

amuk

amuk ii. bedrock

when they camecomewillcome
they mould cerebellae to lust for strip mining
and roads tumbling out in ribbons
from gold mine
to copper mine to bauxite mine
to nickel mines carcinogenic
in the name of 'green transportation'
and palaces in the netherlands, britain, france, portugal
and all in between

*

a tesla owned by an ageing hippie in sacramento
or a french nobleman's summer house
what year is it
it's all export

[ship-shipped-willship]

when we said-say-will say
these plants you destroy or consume
are our relatives
they will laugh
before they burn-burned-willburn them

when we said-say-willsay
these plants are medicinal ancestors
they will laugh
before they stop to burn just long enough
to study and claim—emily blunt in *jungle cruise*—
cures and remedies that they will sell rather than share
that they will in no way recognise as our ancestral own

*

and in the year 2015, centuries after first contact,
when nearly 100,000 children and adults in indonesia alone
are killed by forest fire and smog
they will not be mentioned in the press
orangutans, however, will be mentioned

(the definition of orangutan will also not be mentioned:
orang meaning a person, or peoples in indonesian,
utan meaning forest—
they are our relatives, now, were, will be)

and why our rainforests were ordered to be cut for
wood in amsterdam
keens across the indian ocean,
branched cries heard as wind.

amuk iii. great fires

in the 2010s, i will be on an environmental literature panel
with a white 'nature writer'
who tells me and my caribbean co-panellist
that 'all this was done to make people's lives better.
i'm more worried about brexit than i am about climate change.'

west and east indian, the caribbean co-panellist and i
find ourselves on ocean waves
and our recountings
of brutal enslavement of lands and people
are ignored

'all this was done to make people's lives better.'

[   ]

if you shackle a human's loved ones
and throw them into an abyss

you can take the entire biome
they steward

all this
abyss

*

the flames come-came-willcome in stages

these bonfires their vanities

when independence happens in 1945
[sings] tujuh belas agustus tahun empat-lima

our antecedents rejoice-were rejoicing-willrejoice

but a snake has a particular way of returning
and finding its fangs stuck into the body
of a man who was once
a very poor boy

once in poverty, a condition
only snake-created

soeharto enacted
a poor person's revenge
armed and logistically supported
complete with a lengthy hit list
by western forces

in 1965-'66
a genocide occurs of suspected leftists
including the literal massacre
of what was once the largest feminist movement
in the world

*

marked leftists included labour organisers
and indigenous activists
and gender and sexual and ethnic minorities
and all of these people who wanted
our land-water-air relatives
kept

for us to continue to try to protect

the government is overthrown
and a 33-year-old dictatorship
based on capital and assassination

for more earth for capital—the new order—
into which i was born and in which i was schooled

grounds-ground-willgrind itself into bedrock

*

what happens when all the people who try-tried-willtry
to protect are murdered

this, the ongoing project

on land-and-water relatives from the amazon
to kalimantan

all sweatshop heartache
and mine poisoning
and factory suffocation
and oil rig flares
are this project

are these people
were them, will be

amuk iv. heat rises-rose-willrise in the sky

for them the air has been
calmly surveying a supposed dominion of 'humanity'

for us the air is rageful
the air, our relative, has been fed-feeds-willfeed all our screams

*

in past-present-nearfuture
rainforest is sold
to the same family lines
and this time as 'offsets'
that wash land theft
in shades of saccharine green
again and again and again
by people who will be disbelieved
even after they are killed
for land deeds
as their children are threatened
until the bidding war is won

as an indonesian government worker
is poisoned to death
for seeing the future
and raising a hand to mining blueprints

*

minerals from earth
that should have stayed under
lie across this planet

are communications gathering
and gathering speed through
rock turned digital
in cables underwater

that spark electric fire
and the ways that elements
are drawn into quarters
ultimately spurs us closer to conflagration

and faster and faster
just as earth herself has been led
to turn

to the very end of a five-hundred-year long scream

in this the time future-past-present

its cry persisted-persists-willpersist

amuk [infinity symbol]. waters

place the word **amuk** under
                        the gaseous haze that arises from fire
                        flint-sparked flame
                        on a shallow riverbed
                        under pebbles and earth

the word is changed by every element
wavy in the smoke
trembling under clear water
curved by the weight of stone

the colony has thrown every element at this word

and declared it bent,
the **amok** of dutch, danish and english

                                *

i would like a catchy phrase to describe the twisting of a word into a context that pathologises and derides the original cultures of this word as belonging to psychopaths, then forces those cultures to include this psychopathic description in new dictionaries.

perhaps the word for this should simply be the titular example of it.

let us do some close-reading of wiktionary.org
which is, i am sure, the reason you knew you would definitely
be attending today

*

that website says

amuk
in jawi: اموق (**amuk**)
proto-malayo-polynesian: **amuk**, a cognate of tagalog **hamuk**
and maori **amo**

for remember, now-indonesia was seafaring and trading from
now-australia
for remember, the fern motif
in both maori and minangkabau carvings—

i believe wiktionary.org is correct in this respect, but not with regards to the meaning listed:

they say 'The form *mengamuk* is a reflexive, so it means either "to self-involve in a rage" or "to self-run amok" —

the kind of rage that both a violent keyboard-smashing or a baby might express —

but '**run amok**'
now more often '**run amuck**'
is in itself an anglicisation steeped in bayonets

*

from https://www.etymonline.com/word/amuck:

amuck (adv.)
17c., variant of **amok**; treated as *a muck* by Dryden, Byron, etc., and defended by Fowler, who considered *amok* didacticism.
Entries linking to *amuck*
amok (adv.)

in *run amok* a verbal phrase recorded by 1670s, from Malay (Austronesian) *amuk* "attacking furiously." Earlier the word was used as a noun or adjective meaning **"a frenzied Malay,"** originally in the Portuguese form *amouco* or *amuco*. **[my bold]** There are some of them [Javanese] who ... go out into the streets, and kill as many persons as they meet. ... These are called **Amuco**. ["The Book of Duarte Barbosa: An Account of the Countries Bordering on the Indian Ocean and Their Inhabitants," c. 1516, English translation]
Compare **amuck.**

why would a javanese person—java, both coloniser of other islands
and brutally colonised—be driven to anger.

if someone enslaved your family
including your relatives of animal, mineral,
rivers worshipped and given names,
would your efforts to free them
by killing their captors
be made into a feature film?

*

if you go to the dictionary on the devices many of us including myself have,
from the company named after a fruit
and created from poisonmines-shipping-poisoningfruit-workingtothebrink,

you find

a·mok | əˈmək, əˈmäk | (also amuck)
adverb

PHRASES
run amok (also **go amok**)
behave uncontrollably and disruptively: *the kids are running amok around the house* | *figurative : her feelings seemed to be running amok.*
ORIGIN
mid 17th century: via Portuguese *amouco*, from Malay *amok* 'rushing in a frenzy'. **Early use was as a noun denoting a person in a homicidal frenzy. [my bold-ing]**

the thesaurus that comes with this device:

amok (also amuck)
adverb
PHRASES
run amok
the army had run amok in the town, killing and looting: go berserk, get out of control, rampage, run riot, riot, rush wildly/madly about, go on the rampage; storm, charge; behave like a maniac, behave wildly, behave uncontrollably; become violent, become destructive; go mad, go crazy, go insane; *informal* steam, raise hell; *North American informal* go postal.

*

amuk is a rage that does not necessarily claim victims

turns into:

amok is a homicidal psychopathology
and **to run amuck** is directionless

they have bent our arrows out of shape
words turned misshapen

the bearer of the word **amuk**—
        potentially infants potentially yourselves
has become
either criminal or feral

and there is supposedly
no cause
that one hasever-couldever-willever discern

                *

the army had **run amok** *in the town, killing and looting*

this is, ironically, an appropriate phrase
considering how **amuk**—the original, the rage—
manifests-manifested-willmanifest after hundreds of years of
being made colony

general soeharto leading his army
to a genocide of easily three million
as he keeps and keeps the heart of a boy scarred by poverty
until he has squeezed all inner innocence
ragged

the story of **amuk**'s now-etymology:

'i do not know that there has been a boot over your chest for five hundred years. I do not recognise that this boot is mine, the foot is mine, and that I've rested comfortably on your lower belly as a stool for entire generations over.

and it is your forests i have obliterated to concrete. and it is your nation-state's debt i have held over the peatlands as incentive to choke your own selves with industrial smog in order to emulate us, the genesis of **amuk**.

i do not recognise the presence of other tenses in every tense.'

*

the gall of pathologising **amuk**
is the journey through languages it's been molded to
through macheted etymology

until a meaning implying 'mass unrest
like a civil war' [as natives will bicker]
joins the indonesian ministry of education's
dictionary itself
as the first entry

the second entry in our official dictionary
also denotes murder as outcome
'in the context of certain cultural activities.'

in the official indonesian dictionary

amuk as emotion
the baby-rage, self-consuming fire,
ur-meaning
is not listed

in its stead, the third meaning in our dictionary for amuk:

a psychological term referring to 'an uncontrollable condition;
a riot with violence'

*

the story of **amuk**
is that of tongues being swallowed whole
and ever-quietening forests

suddenly, their heads awake
when the smoke has finally reached their nostrils
after hundreds of years

when the waterline threatens
their bedframes sourced from now-corporate lands

*

and they cry 'humanity!' ad nauseam
'this crisis is humanity's fault'
'something wrong with humanity'

but they would be saying that,
wouldn't they

we were never supposed to be human

time and again, at work,
i am complimented on my anger

my last gig before the first lockdown,
i was told on a bright stage by a former world leader,
having just pointed out that 'plant trees!'
does not include how palm oil trees
in plantations built on rainforest ash
are poison writ large:

'i love your rage'

*

the echo of it
throughout continued indigenous genocide
like a valley girl chasing after me

'**i** love your rage'
'i **love** your rage'
'i love **your** rage'
'i love your **rage!**'

i love your rage . i love your rage .

as though it is a painting
or a one-woman show
but perhaps to them, it is [was, will be]
all these words ever are

is this what i'm doing here in england
over and over again, just

—'here's some rage for you to maybe love'—

before the stage dims
and we retreat to our homes

*

the shame of hearing this
that immediately bleeds into the rage
once someone says they love it [on stage]
[which stages]

this blade is a prop! it is said to my face, turning warm

no, says the blade

if these living words did not exit into rivers of others' rages
in communion
they would gnaw at my fascia
i know this

and in addition, it is unuseful to fret
about how anger is framed
when you know the stakes and plays
of the game

*

what does it mean to be praised for feeling fire

why must we relay a litany of genocides
to try to spark a pinprick of empathy
in silk-cocooned minds

running **amuk** interference
in an age of metals turned surveillance

anger creates spheres of force
planetary geneses

creates DSM-worthy crimes out of
words' innocence

*

and what is said to run **amuck**?

children
farm animals
those with cognition not recognised
as being herd-approved

bodies undulating in riots—hooligans
—thugs bearing disrespect on the move

no logical causality for
unless to prove the cause is illogic

the threat of **amuckness**
lest rules laid down
by enlightenment presumptiousness
are allowed to be hammered in
—fence posts
—corrals
—barbed wire
and skin

*

your beloved walks into a black hole
unable to move their limbs
and you hear a splash

you rush with your fists against the black hole
it tells you there was-is-willbe no beloved
if there was-is-willbe it is-was-willbe happy
and there was-is-willbe no waters, not a drop

so you must have been mistaken
and why are you **running amuck**?

through most recent prior centuries,
amuk is absorbed into european vernacular.
[dutch danish portuguese   english]

I LOVE YOUR RAGE is all the rage.
THEY LOVE OUR RAGE.

it suits the civilising mission.

it suits terra nullius terraforming.

*

voice-voices of amuk:

in a sense, it is a resounding victory that you have not been able to capture our-my essence, to pawn-havepawned-beabletopawn these four letters as another word for storefronts and amnesiac thesauri.

in a sense, it is indeed a tactical triumph that you do not-didn't-willnot know where my fire lies. that your satellite maps, hungry for new ground, regard our-my combustion into flames as flailing, lacking direction.

each element feels the presence of
and is the presence of **amuk**
each animate and seemingly inanimate thing
the stones feel **amuk**
the bones, above ground and below

they feel it with us
so none rage alone

*

there are secret, sacred homes
hidden in planets across linguistic cosmologies
(so complex they baffle string theory)
where **amuk** is felt, cradled, nurtured
as a seething that encourages delight
guffaws
a holding of each other
—beyond certain maritime holds—
into self-made wooden boats
to glide across rivers
reimagined as clean, serene, ours
to violently dismantle infrastructures of disbelief
to spit on a force field
and watch it crumble

to rage not for display
to rage not for a sucking into the matrices of acceptable emotion
to rage beyond respectable castle yonder
to rage beyond 'third world' 'underdeveloped' 'left-behind'
to rage beyond gilded names for fictitious crimes and fictitious capital
to rage beyond our own skin's acquiescing to the audience
in order to survive

*

there are whole universes in which **amuk** does not mean death

in these interpretations, **amuk**

                                              means

sahabat-sahabat,

kita hidup—we were alive
                        we are alive

                                        we live

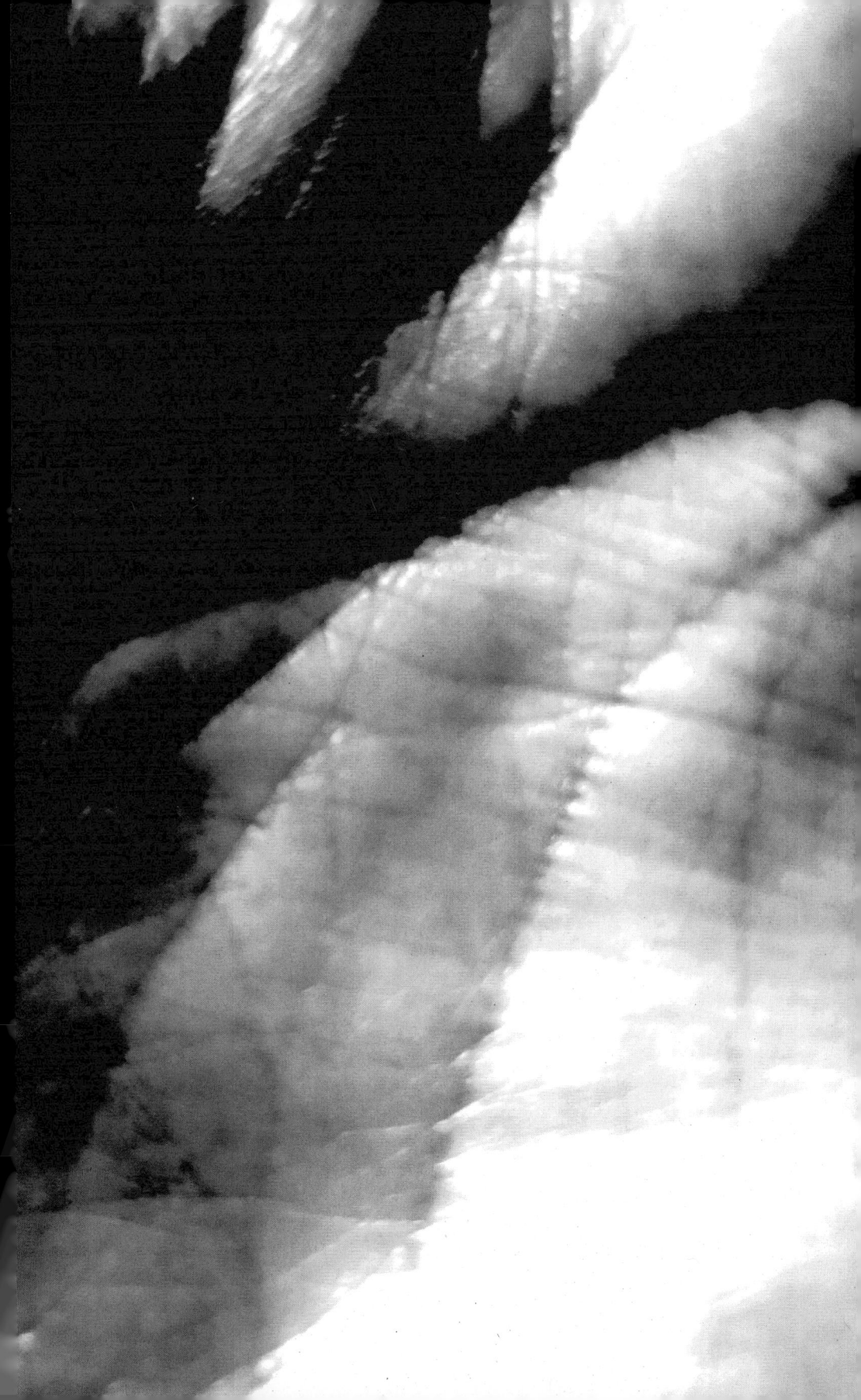

*to write them means
they are no longer
prayers but are now animals.
Other people can hunt them.*

       In our time-travel cosmology of language

       in which

       we are always in multiple frameworks of time by virtue
       of having no past-present-future tenses

       my small tendrils envelop the words.

                  Reverse.

Cradle hunted words, turn them towards a state of prayer;

the words are quietly chanting themselves into supplication.

Into clothing themselves as the unsurveilled.

The exhaling, breathing words

in alphabets hunters do not detect—

there will always be too much to possibly capture

if we do not name everything.

The beasts say they are prayers.

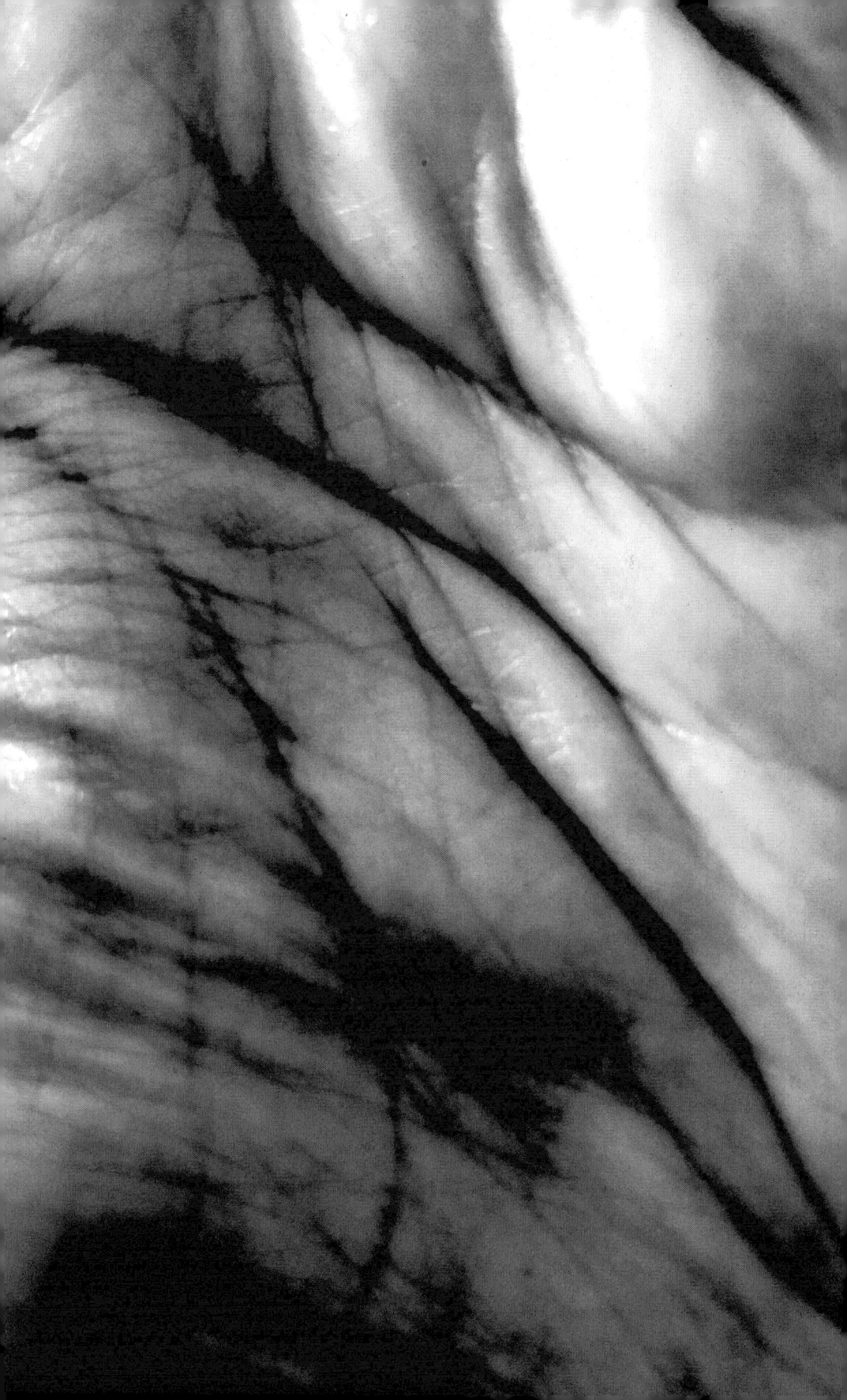

II. doa

or, what is reached for

withstanding is a prayer

pain is a prayer, the soulbody screeching

it asks for help in the guise of fire

amuk is a prayer

is a word that prays

and is itself a unit of asking

prayer is a form of rage

while you rage, remember to keep the truth

      within these arms: [   ]

prayer directed at x

after serpentwithfeet

keep me tender in cupped hands

let dust turn back to felt,
cuts beget blooming,
arias from nail-bitten mouths

you can't take me anywhere
udah lama
let us stay here buttering dreams
in a genocidal neighborhood

keep me tender in there
keep me sleepywarm

freshly bathed as algos close in
for coin, raucousrock of death
could be any year

don't ever tell them where i am
where you cup me quiet
and teething again

rub cajuput oil on my
miniature back,

and when they ask
what you have there say
you're praying

prayer against the hunt

within these flights, a cypseline spell to clasp
inward inward, a held asking

chanting known only to bloodstream
its edges a lipid barrier

come hold where the songbirds
swell and blot outwards from the chest

keep an incantation sacred
though it be on the page, possessed

in the way a spirit comes into a body, not
as stamped value for circulation

belonging to none but the feeling of belonging
when all the cells calm as one—home, unhateful

to cleanse in reeds

my mother, a child, walks to the spring
and rubs her body with wet grasses.
she is taught, she learns
a scrubbing of detritus realm
from our barrier of selves.

the bending of wills and heads
has not yet led to pesticidal lathering.
my grandfather has not yet installed
the house's waterways, aqua as bended will
and not will to enter, to bathe in no more than.

these waters from which direction
erupts, the cause for no such
words as *north south east west*
used in our village before—
there is only upstream, downstream.

this couplet all the world needs to know
of divining place and ways within it:
where to wash in a known rush of sluice,
what part of the earth to bring
to skins. how to gentle a renewal,

how to be smallness and cold, to begin.

prayer for cave with rectangular light

ricochet of particles laced with waves a crochet clackety, darkness-grave.

another day complains you moved alone too many times today

(and this was before a pandemic of stops and starts to graze late capital's elbows)

and those old thoughts: if only i could turn a window into the ship that brought uwo on hajj

and if bed could be cloud and then menyublim, into another bed in jakarta

and the walls open up into themselves as mirrored in southern hemisphere

and the shape of a kite in electric wires tells you where stalagmites are now

stalactites, the jaws of a stone home turned the green of creeping branches

there, your mother humming 'burung camar'

tub

what digs you out with a verdigris scalpel, while a powerful blast ignited in their latest attempt to grow lives in the dirt of your online receipt, human blood carries all kinds of filigreed debris, coexisting with the coffin hinges from grotesquely groping eyes panoptic that brought you your morning kettle-hiss, faucet fiddling now, let loose, hotness   coldness, piety, lust, bewilderment, supremacy writ into capital, rent hikes for men oiling hair with your rainforests, corners hiding gaspings for breath, a ladybug swatted away by a tank in gaza, a man with down's syndrome killed with no consequences, violet memories of neuropathic pain still imprinted on your body you are soaking in a fluid warm enough to let it bleed out, breathe in, deliberately feel the edges of a ghost, the heart already drawn in pencil on your hospital radiator seven years ago, fuzzy twinges bear on your muscle feel these deliberate, you may not bathe in kind waters so lower your head below the surface, part your lips and scream it

(before firewood prays, she hears)

a burning woman makes a shitty comrade
the smoke's cumbersome, fire a safety hazard

so what if the firemen gagged her with a gasoline rag, so—
they slit her with a lighter and threatened any decibels

on the arboreal gurney. enough times of facing angry shouts
for screaming, the sapling lost the ability to verbalise flames 'appropriately'

for branches to remain 'appropriate' requires time's reversal
and denial of how often she bursts into the mouth of a star

why go back and back there, for kicks?
why spread an inferno to flooding steppes

black clouds look like breath, her knifing chest
no longer understands a divide of sky and flames

tug an ash braid. see if it's god in there,
the one her mother said lives inside her with the blades

lex talionis

let's not hurt a living thing; instead, make mirrors bleed cut glass / slit wooden doorways with claw marks / unleash grass' maws and bring water / to where it's been scarcified by board members' stock options / slave barons' architectural legacies worth / more than ever apologising / to a single disabled person forced to use historic stairs when we should not / i want the windows to rock themselves back and forth / at night in their own bathrooms / i want intercoms to ring with first-person accounts / of access abuse from morning to night / supernaturally / i want the floors to be gloopy and jello / and carry disabled people from one end to the other, even through sky / the floors will not work for anyone else / and will not work for disabled white people who shit on the 'third world' / it won't stop until the collectively scarred say *that's enough now that's enough* / i say that too often, keeps happening / i'm gloopy jello rage-numbed and don't give a flying fuck / fiancé has heard me panic attack at least once / for each minute of the twenty-four-hour gregorian day / how bad do you want our flesh to implode until you have faith / until building can empathise / relate it to the feeling of apportioned stones and concrete and plexiglass inside of one's veins / of one's years without prescribed painkillers for recurrent 'level ten' pain / and with the elephant's glut i'm now on / even 'dulled' amount is red-glazed, boil-infused / not sure what i bit down on before / not sure if i can keep trying to bite down anymore / i know i have enough inside to stay alive but the buildings / who are also people / say *eat shit sayonara bai baiiiiii* / every time it happens, reminds me how it used to be / a scar opening just enough to be back and back there / there too and back / (not trauma porn, just a soul trying to type / in lieu of throwing pillows at a midnight wall) / how badly do you want us to paint / the scent of endless streets and sidewalks we crouched on / fell upon / pebbles rise to meet our skins / seeds gasp in comprehension / do you know how it feels to chronicle still / the causes of one's own survivor-dom / not have it absorb into people until / they see your limbs change shape your mind bust open your right eye close / iceberg tip of our agonies / unpeeled / and i almost want to laugh watching them / would rather spit in their eye than hear again / as though they're original / a chorus line stretching in infinite memory / vibrato / 'i didn't know it was that bad'

peace, with c-ptsd

what are set preparedness actions
in case of a bed of petals over quicksand,
as gravity's nature plus time is tasked
with doing to glittering feathers and sprightly bones

could be no,
to the visions—

a violent refusal is often necessary,
the high-wattage flashlight in the cave

don't remember *the descent*
and how the women all died in wounds
befitting their mortal flaws—

the younger sister breaking free on her own
to a death suspended and miles from surface
the elder sister ripped in the guts
wet viscera spill of her riotous mourning

perhaps if i bundle up in calm,
many years in the future, i'll die
at rest and at ease, in a dream
where everyone's here and there was no need
for all the tension cramping a soulbody

hoping the caving in would one day
turn it diamond turn it forgiven
turn it forgetting turn it a giving

prayer doa in which di mano: english inggris, baso minang and dan bahasa indonesia fight berseteru

karena dia merasuki semua seperti kesurupan bahasa inggris

    karena dia mengambil jantung syair dan menjadikannya

terjemahan untuk bisnis

        onde mande

    apo nyenyo inggris iko?   la laruik sanjo

        dan kampuang

·   di mato inggris dak tontuuuuu lai

karena dia mengambil pantun dan menjadikannya pantoum

    they don't understand

pantun weaves weddings and mourning rituals together

        as they teach 'pantoum' in a classroom

    and do not even say our names

        he fashions your camera lens

        to the setting of white tourist

bukan dia yang mengayomimu   ayo

        ambo bundo

        sini sayang   kurangkul selalu

excuse me—

        jangan ke situ

prayer encased in my father's vision of a journey to the afterlife

he says it like *we have entered the next stop*

awaiting our turn to board the choo-choo.

we're here now at a stop, and they have gone

on to beyondland. you might as well purchase a snack,

kiss a baby on the cheek, hide the meat cleavers

from clumsy fingers. hum along to the singing clouds,

the only ones who seem to know routes.

this orchestration of transport, inefficient,

smothered in tangled grief, a spider's spinning torso.

connecting regrets from caboose to caboose.

my father declares these are but distractions,

the tracks are laid out in permanent ink.

and his mother and father await at a station

so hoped for and thought of, it bears no signage

when one steps out—unriven and gladsome,

chests a sonorous basso, the air blaring glory,

buoyant in burnished praise—and onto its lighted plane.

for a jakarta microbiome

because do calls this house an ecosystem
where straddling folioles tangle mighty-fisted
along a wire canopy he strung
above the brick-and-pot garden, and city fox
coming like a client for bananas they feed it sunny
and rats on rare occasion, 'because this is an ecosystem',
while i'd lie, wide-eyed for a tail out the window
and up there explosions of birdstrain, as though not far there isn't
vast crackling chemical dust in convoys of exhaust
and here where industrious mosquitoes venture against
the pop! of electric tennis racket and worm eggs
are down-the-drained with soap and warm water
that comes from a tap (unlike when i was small,
and we were servants to boiling for safety,
enjoying waves of wait, billowing slower breaths into ease)
and there by your room the aloe row that mo
breaks open with reverence to soften her hair
and when i was small, when you were a baby,
we'd wait for baygon to be sprayed in each room
and would open the doors and sniff, no timer
and safe to come in when the chemsmell lifted,
but now an earthy dispelling of such things
for the humans, bracts inside who mould the way
the weight of the house and its inhabitants
all prayed for, making this green
a node of the world

tsunami warning, facing shore

samudra:

      would-be glass-smasher,
mystic, crystallising
rhythm to granular form on ripple-lakes.

      my body an inner gravel.

on a landing stories-high,
so close to spray it nauseates volcanic,
      sumatra's face meets the roil,

and i cannot look upwards—
though i know we mere insani, sandlocked,
have detected the waters
      lifting their fist.

look at me who has always loved you
and don't strike now.
don't strike.

the truth is in remembering waves
that feel like blue-gray air
      about to turn,

      to make sea-cloud graves,
and vast sky cut from upturned basins,

heaven's lip, blooming purple into salt.

prayer for man in accident, elephant and castle

six metres away from a charnel bike
you lie with closed lids beneath sky of brick,

blessing a forest of gravel, helmet on and face up.
three of the rubberneckers on 999 calls,

and by your brown solemnity,
the towers of people living out a dreamers' ending

of others' displacement, where smoke would hit
their new build windows that same bruised week,

from the station fire, nowhere that wealth
could possibly cocoon from this:

your body and your family,
what prayers slam against.

prayer as fistful of praise

dear blood, i remember

your child arms, and our father,

propping me up on a sidewalk

on our way home from wretched hospital

in a foreign squawk of city.

my memory is cloud of protection,

i do not recall most life in great detail.

it is all there, contained under a breath

of haze, a smothered dulling of incision.

i apologise again for worry,

and thank you for the qur'an

that you kept close and reread, retread,

then gave to me when i left again.

these are prayers in return;

in prayer, we revisit understanding

steadfastness of kin. dodo says

'brainwaves are non-local'

for the seventy-hundredth time.

i believe him because i know:

you seem calm, from afar.

i will return your child-limbs'

help to me, return how you've carried me

up the stairs at home, as i carried you

when a very small child, shrieking

until the night i told you a story.

preceding a prayer for the dead asian men who inspired *a nightmare on elm street*

americana churns a grist of slashes
and fear of the faces it burns

spits out a recurring broadcast of freddy
on screens in formation, grenade-fuelled

having claimed that if you slept
you'd die unwaking, you fled

rose to an observatory height

watching as agent orange
held tight to blood molecules

as the bombs that made you run
to a cold stretch of states

continued to bloom death
in home soils that noticed you depart
as mines and sweatshops back home
were squeezed for gleaming suburbs

that continue to laugh at the accents
with which you prayed, to avoid
terror under empire-moon

as suited men determined
these present, pixeled mausolea

where hollow memory-conscribers
confined traces of your bones
to blades seeking ingenue flesh

where are your hands in this celluloid
and how were they positioned

the overseers grasped at, sought to break
your minds' eye
in a cycle of VHS-led obliteration

vastly beyond any vengeance
your sleep could imagine

flinging the cause of your desperate leaving
to an unfurling exploit
of further nightmares

[*A Nightmare on Elm Street* was inspired by reports in the 1980s of dozens of Southeast Asian men in the US—refugee men in particular, who had fled from Laos, Vietnam, and Cambodia, and especially those from Hmong communities—dying in their sleep, with many having reported nightmares. Medical professionals called this Sudden Unexplained Nocturnal Death Syndrome (SUNDS).]

a cartographic hunger

on the hours is a mapping of bodily reminders, of how
        there are cupped hands of laughter and continuance

     in this country where gold filling spits on new bones,
          gnashes femurs caught in a border's wire,
               infects us with acid-accented matter
    detritic in waves of lithium and copper

how do we pay no attention to this country

          hone breath to build for another land
    [in the same coordinates of space]

how do we forget this landscape of traps
    filling reservoirs with disbelieved wounds
all hyperspeed-harvested, cultured
    to feed a mythic line's open mouth

      we sit reminding each other
          how kids across continents were born fleeing,
              entering living with the shock of a new universe

as sails woven from gold's price
cover our dead where they rest,
spanned lives an internal marble
          glowing in the spleen

      we are building other countries,
    astonishing names permeating
        the cracked shores we wake to

the countries we seek have been self-constructing—
    adhesive to each other in quiet clearings
    when nightfall is breath at a time

        tiny plenitudes
        handfuls of open waters
       plain resuscitations in sleep

the countries we weave
    in secret karst

candid punchlines they missed the first time
    palms on palms on backs of bodies
    rubbing softly
    humming a heat

        oceanic measurement
   in seams they thought ripped
        intricate philosophies millennia ahead

          and who has the time to translate for them
   we who are ever untranslating to free
    the epically innate

keeping house, reaching for names
    for genders hunted to whispers,
        clearing hearth for formations
sensed first as pulse

welcoming the practice of inhalation
an intake of possible ships against ships

       see ancient traders praying
            a sussuration of bismillahs
see melanated medieval

       profound anchoring in the seeds
           transported from archipelago
   to archipelagic ends

plague years make breathing heavy
     quick
     nightmare horse plowing clouds of insomnia

      looking up to the undersides of billionaire bunkers
  thousands of words for rainforests
picture-framed as carbon credit scams

      look up further, to indigenous firmament—

feel air swimming down our gullets
      touch aloe on the skin that stings
from pylons they've tried to graft in seamless

     touch only immediacy
       of exhale
        to wake these countries

     teaching ourselves their escape—
showing in each other the joyfully absconding
     breathing an entreaty for space

       hailing slow timekeepers
    who understand everything
       believe each story

       cut their profiles from air
       a chiselled grace

prayer for dzikir as mnemonic device

still all your percussive orbits
and soft-click a thumb
to each third
of each finger

praise
how light
work is, unshirking
remembrance

vicissitudes plant grief
in skin-pricks,
out of the gasping sun
climbs daybreak

crackling, cyclonic
core tenets and ninety-nine names
flooding back
to thick bloodstream

memento mori, recuerda tu vida
ingat, ingat,
        ingat-ingat

matrihaemoglobin

i.

i will not bear children, my hips wide and unyielding;

our arms, rivers of bloodline.

minangkabau—world's largest matrilineal society,

our continuation, padusi.

our joys, bundles of infants.

the choice to unmother in one way is a choice to mother other things.

is a choice for one body to extend the luck of breath.

stopping medication during pregnancy,

how would baby bear the pain i've learned to river,

how could i welcome a soul to womb with toxic shock,

how would i propel us both through eugenicist clouds blocking airpipes

to recklessly induce another life, when bloodline

is asking me, eons of padusi in mitochondrial chorus,

back and back and back:

'onde mande, la laruik sanjo.

makin lamo hiduik,

makin banyak diraso.'

ii.

the land belongs to the minang woman.

more rarely said: the land is inside us.

i hoard the rustling quietude of tanah datar fish ponds.
pandemic-besieged in a flat in south london,
i close my eyes to the beat of bedug and the laughter
of thunder-voiced girls aged eighteen to eighty,

in rumah gadang lintau buo.

once, on a village visit, my brother

met a woman working in paddy fields

who said she'd held our uwo as a baby.

how could this land not be in our mouths

our glands, stoked granular whims, our legs

bathed in instinct, our hair thick and braided

my lost ones are soil embedded in skin

are the breadth of breathwork across rapid straits

are the way of return, the weight of migration

turned satchel that fits in the hand, compared to

the borderless country that lives molecular

speaking to vast populations of daughters

and bending oxygen into the forests

alive in our raucous eyes, the life ahead.

prayer for baby breath

a friend and i talk rainforest infernos,
how she'd had hope
for that failed carbon scheme
that i'd always known to be
core of ash, not white hope
for land, because in that scheme
indigenous was nowhere & hope's
an indescribable hue.

my friend had reported
from scorch apocalypse.
all the children choking
on ashes of ancient holy growing,
parents bent down, evicted, having sold
land to whoever paid those men
with relentless fists, then the call came—
the west needed coverage: orangutans.

the cameraman was furious—
tens of thousands of people
with burning lungs who would
not meet the next night,
afraid they knew it.
orangutans.

we love orangutans more than they know,
word meaning people/s of forest/s;
but they love orangutans more than us
(when to us we are both root-entangled).
& in the end, who holds as much forest grief
for the woman whose baby was gasping.

the baby got coverage.
so did an orangutan.

this poem is for that infant,
who did not survive
what erases newborns of all kinds
from bark they belong to,
by suffocating their bronchioles with it.

with all of it.

doa angin / wind prayer

1.

swell intracellular pathways with dust-sprinkled light.

heave that cloud brigade right into my lungs, young cunning.

open up worlds with obliteration of shadow at smallest smirk.

gun for warm honey of sun's tongue upon persistent skins.

glow internal organs up and up 'til the throat catches shining.

contagious, hungry sheen of luminescence upon the bones of feet.

breath as a gentle lustre switch, gusting to and fro.

anyway the air blows, peace gleams: a lake cut by the moon.

sky inside all of us, recreated with exhalation.

our mouths catch the tail end of the stratosphere.

bring stars into my gullet with the next few inhales,

let me escape this world's grating butchery, painlessly immolating

threat to limbs with cold fire of space, by vault of heaven.

i trip into gust of sour lung

toxin-refracted dust makes for
neon sun-dipping, by and by

night comes on, a dirt blanket
for all the 'developed' to rejoice at spoils

inhale how free the stratosphere
thinks we are, its grief

a lullaby in your throat, its shriek
is humming a cavern to trembling

shape of an entreaty

to begin a zephyr,
there needs to be an indecayable,
knotted place
of help to hold onto;

then the flag of air
may be drawn,

an undulating black thread
going over pages of cloud,
then turning into
the very book of them

until the moon unfurls
in a storm's illusion
as just below, our frames
are whip-buffeted into blades of grass
made more alive
by air's capricious intention

theories for sky

at sunset, we are sediment
bottom-feeding
in a cup of honey ginger tea

tonight the kidnappers forgot
they'd left scissors in our tent
with which we poke stars through

if the firmament is weeping
it should know there are plenty to witness it
clothes of whole provinces soaked in its mess

we could be inside so many snow globes
frozen water on our tongues
land prepared to be tipped on its head

clouds and estuaries
are long-distance
steadily converging in billions of bodies

        air entering
        breath leavening

        grey, primordial ghosts of water
        nesting patient in a newborn lung

dust ablution

spreading fingers against a wall then onto self,
what cleansing's reachable when spent,
followed by what supposedly-holy movements can.

salvation comes from trying
and wanting god as much as from
calmer tendon stretch, from anti-affirmation of what,

to much of venal world, a good body should
a good body can a good body best
a best body as though heaven's narrow-gauged

and god a headmistress rapping rulers against
these many best bodies not marked so by others,
against totalities given to her beneficence.

doa tanah / dirt prayer

lower me rooted,
soil-breasted.

iridescent, brown,
calm with earthworms.

meeting maker at ground level,
lying straight, agog in peat.

toes wrapped in tender shoots,
shoulders fertile with moonlight.

horizon-wide hips
in paddy field blessing.

rhythmic hands tapping *dry season*
wet season dry season wet —

tomorrow's another warm betting ground,
a place-based faith in no lost state.

legs sludging off a gash of chemicals,
hoping mine-makers weep their blood

for a change. the sunrise a mouth
of glowing clay, greets mineral

selves we are as its own cubs.
caulking our joints

with the love of other bodies,
flesh as rainforest and rice, endless.

Notes

Amuk means 'rage/to rage' in Indonesian and Malay. European colonists translated anger—of peoples, of biomes, in response to slavery, environmental destruction, and land theft—as frenzied, indiscriminate homicide, the origin of the concept in English of 'running amok'.

'DSM' refers to the *Diagnostic and Statistical Manual of Mental Disorders*, published and updated by the American Psychiatric Association. An example of how horrific and societally-contingent its contents can be: in the first edition in 1952, homosexuality was classified as a mental disorder.

doa: prayer / prayers.

Acknowledgments

Thank you, thank you, thank you to the readers.

Many thanks to the editors and publishers of the following journals and anthologies, in which poems from this collection were previously published, at times in earlier forms:

About Place Journal, Here Was Once the Sea: An Anthology of Southeast Asian Eco-Writing (University of Hawai'i Press), *Cordite Poetry Review, GRANTA, harana poetry, How We Hold: Rehearsals for Art and Social Change* (Serpentine Galleries Press), *How We Reclaim & Commemorate: An Anthology of Multilingual Poetry and Poetics* (University of Hawai'i Press), *Kweli Journal, Massachusetts Review, Ploughshares, Poetry London, The Rialto, Altered States* (Ignota Press), *Stand, Tupelo Quarterly, Venti Journal, Zocalo Public Square*.

Works cited: *OBIT,* Victoria Chang, Copper Canyon Press, 2020.
'Bad Translation', by Elisa Taber, in *Violent Phenomena: 21 Essays on Translation*, ed.s Kavita Bhanot and Jeremy Tiang, Tilted Axis Press, 2022.
Bayo Akomolafe quoted in 'We aren't "in control" of climate crisis', an interview with him conducted by Ruby Russell and Sarah Mewes, *Deutsch Welle*, July 7, 2020.

Thank you to Edinburgh Futures Institute and Ioannis Kalkounos for commissioning *AMUK* as a performance for the Climate Futures Initiative. Thank you to the National Centre for Writing, particularly Peggy Hughes, for support that gave me time and space to write.

Jane Commane, it is as ever an immense joy and honour to work with you—thank you so much for understanding, for poetic midwifery. Thank you to Angela Hicken for all your work supporting us poets at Nine Arches. Thank you very much to my agent Abi Fellows, who helps bring precious things to fruition, with purpose.

Thank you to my family, who are dearly loved, including my brother, to whom this book is dedicated. Thank you to my husband, for all the many ways you bring peace to my life, and to his loving family. Deep gratitude to so many artists in different mediums, whose work aided and inspired me. Thank you to my friends for mutual support, and to my creative communities for welcoming me into the fold. In particular, I'd like to shout out my fellow members of the Shadow Heroes Translators' Collective, my fellow contributors to *Violent Phenomena: 21 Essays on Translation* (Tilted Axis), and the transnational crip/chronic illness community of artists I am proud to be a part of.

More gratitude to translators and linguistic experts: to Hēmi Kelly — and to Jeffrey Zuckerman for connecting us — who shared with me the usage of 'amo' in Te Aka, the Māori dictionary. Thank you to Eric Abalajon for connecting me to Ramon Guillermo, who in turn kindly shared with me the usage of the cognate 'hamok' in Filipino. Thank you, Ramon. Hēmi and Ramon have made me feel even more strongly that our peoples are strands of the same cloth, across oceans, that words *can* travel respectfully, against a colonial otherwise; I hope the readers feel this too.

This book was completed amidst multiple genocides occurring in the world, stemming from colonial capitalism, from Palestine to Papua, from Sudan to Congo. It is written with amuk in solidarity with the survivors and victims of these genocides.

In the process of writing these poems, several beloved people in my life left this plane of existence. To them I humbly say: thank you, I miss you, and I wish we had had more time; part of writing *amuk* has been a self-reminder that time is non-linear, and that our cosmologies allow us to always be meeting again.

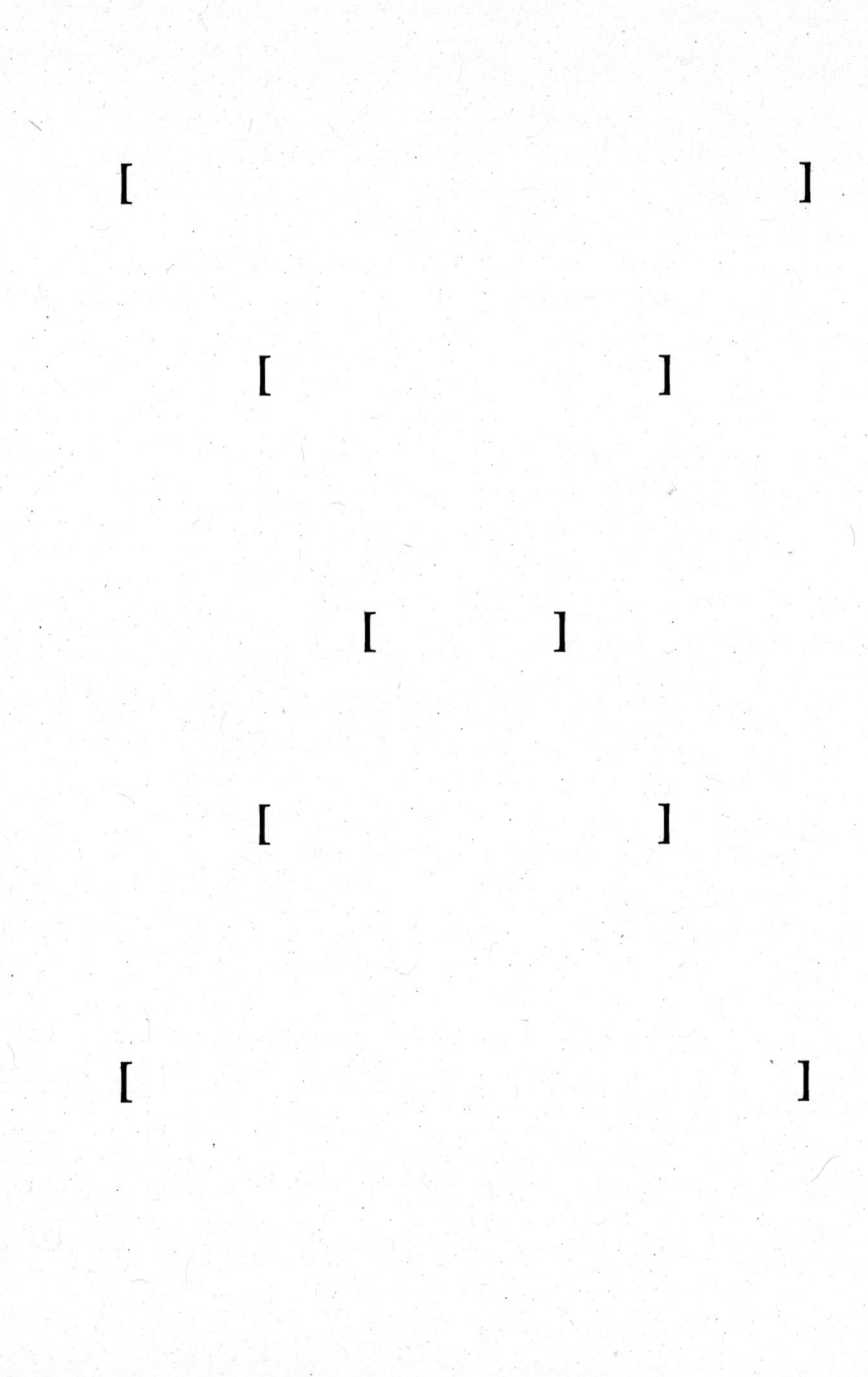

Cover Description

Against a chartreuse background, 'amuk' is written in black cursive, inside two brackets. Above the title in the right-hand corner, in the same hand: the word 'amuq' in Jawi script, under which is the Filipino cognate 'hamok' written as 'ha-mo' in Baybayin, and underneath that is the Māori cognate 'amo' written in the Latin alphabet.

Large, black brackets also surround the blurb on the back cover.

Further image descriptions:
p.63 black and white photograph of the left palm of a hand
p.65 black and white photograph of the right palm of a hand

Cover art and further images by Khairani Barokka.